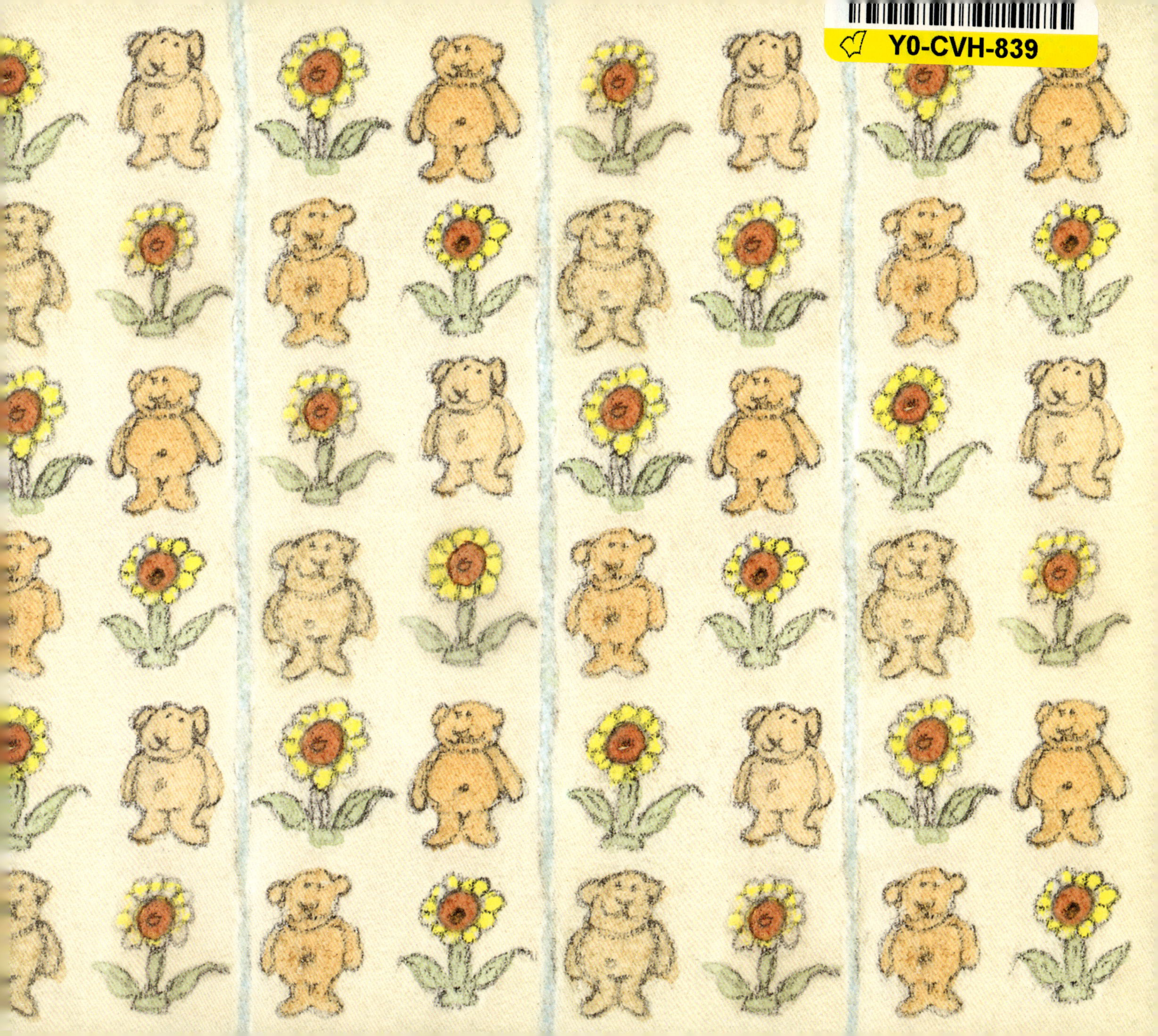

Bears

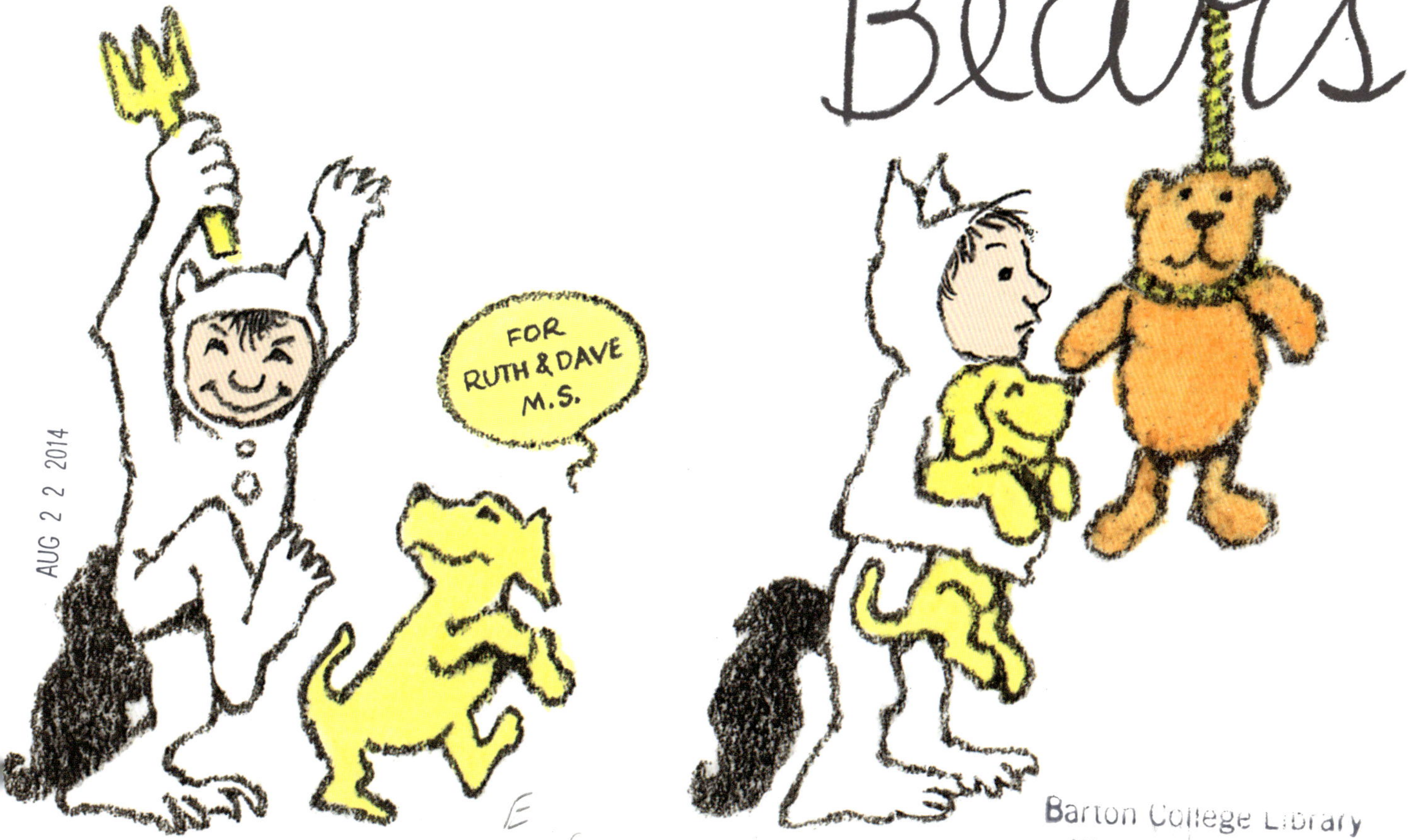

story by Ruth Krauss
pictures by Maurice Sendak

Bears

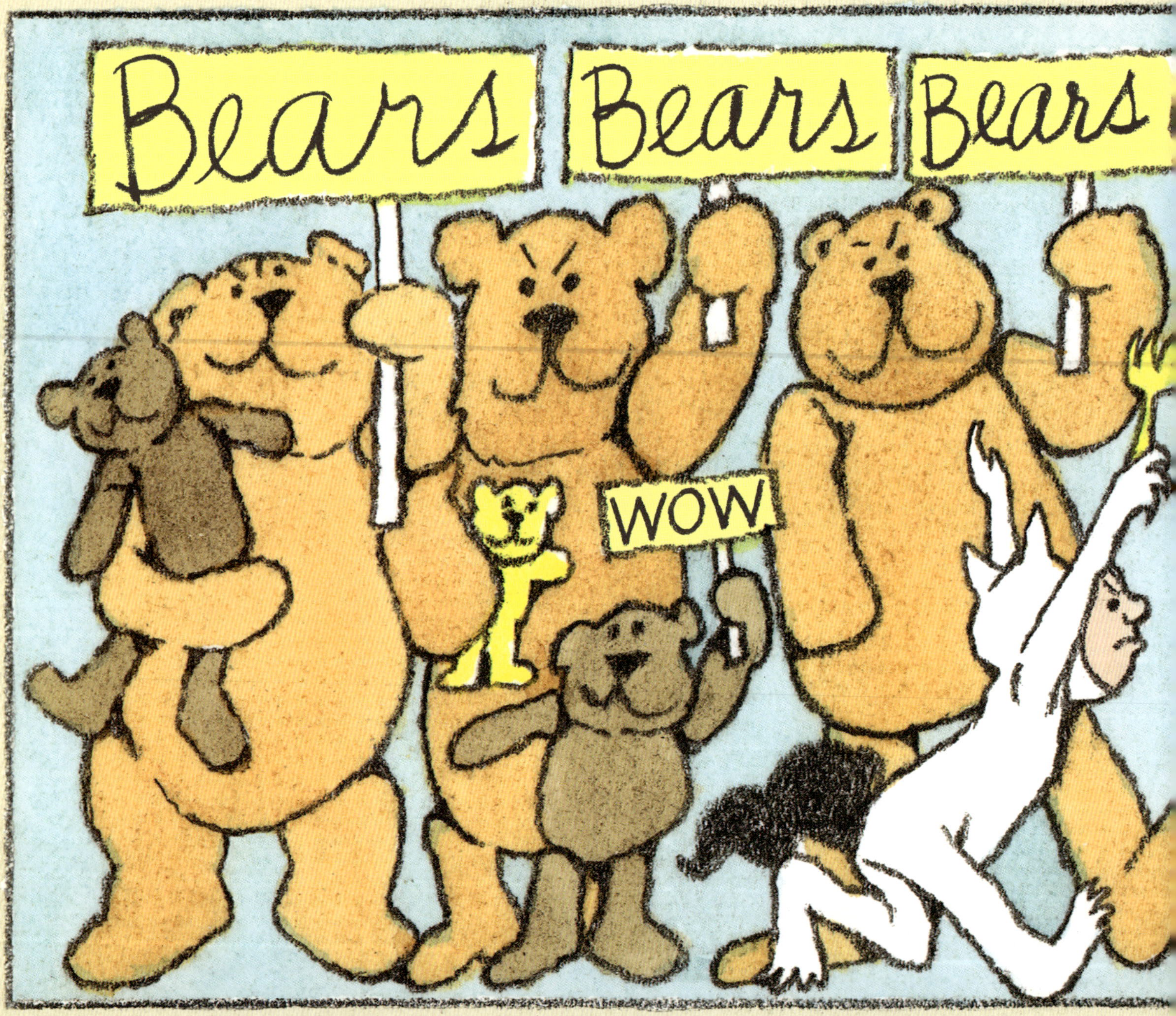
Bears
Bears
Bears
WOW

Bears Bears GRRR

On the stairs

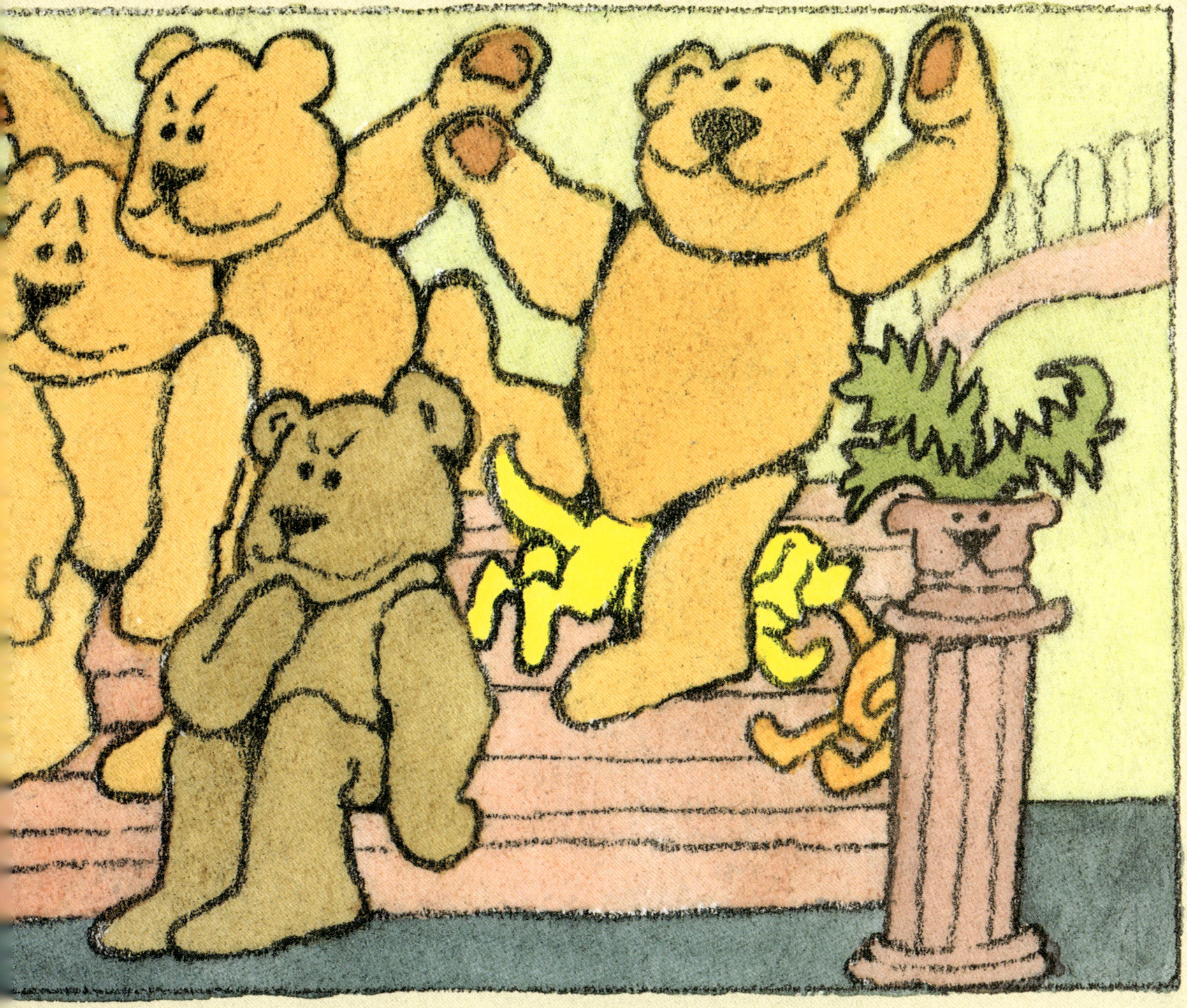

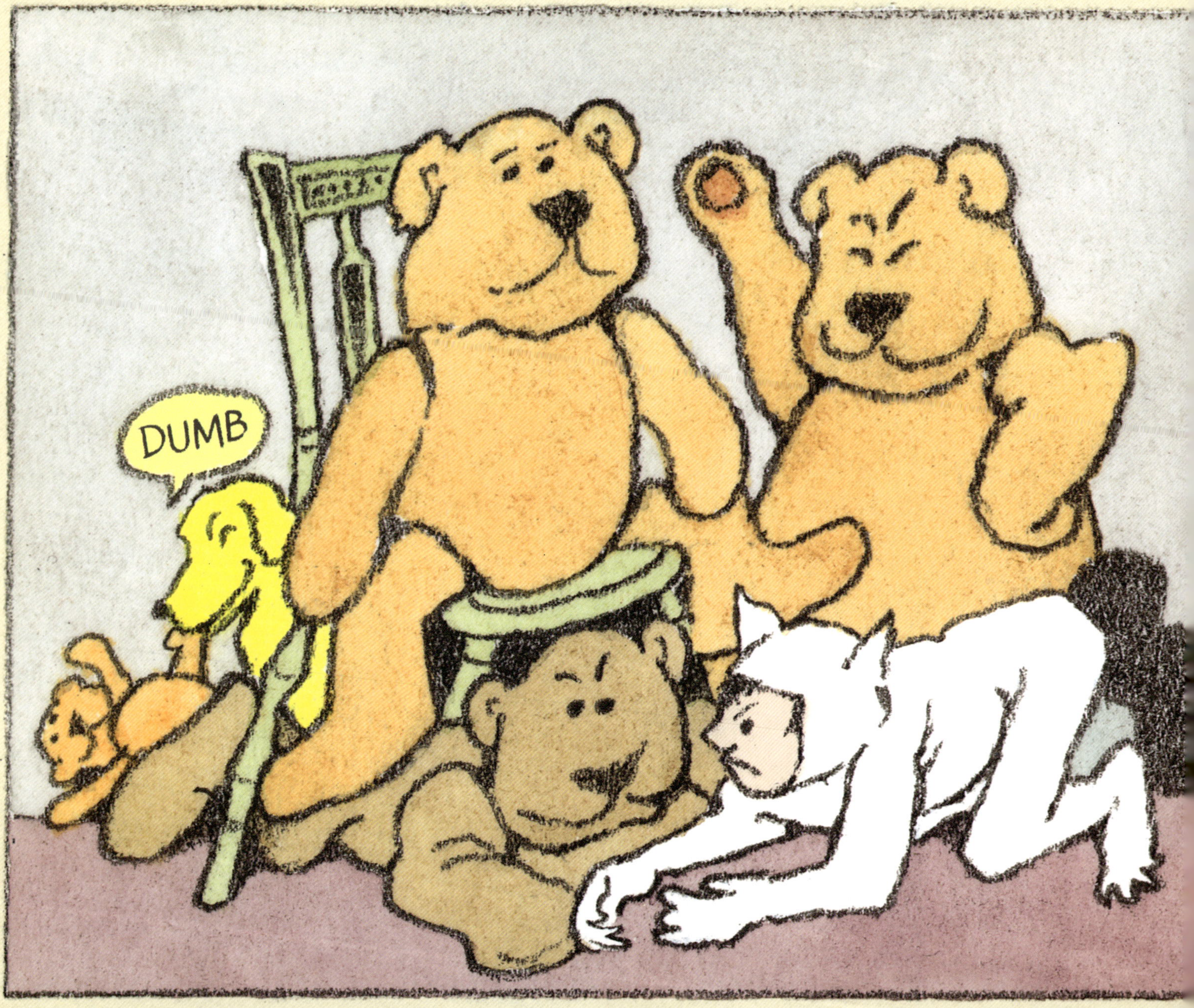
DUMB

Under chairs

HELLO?

Washing hairs

HA

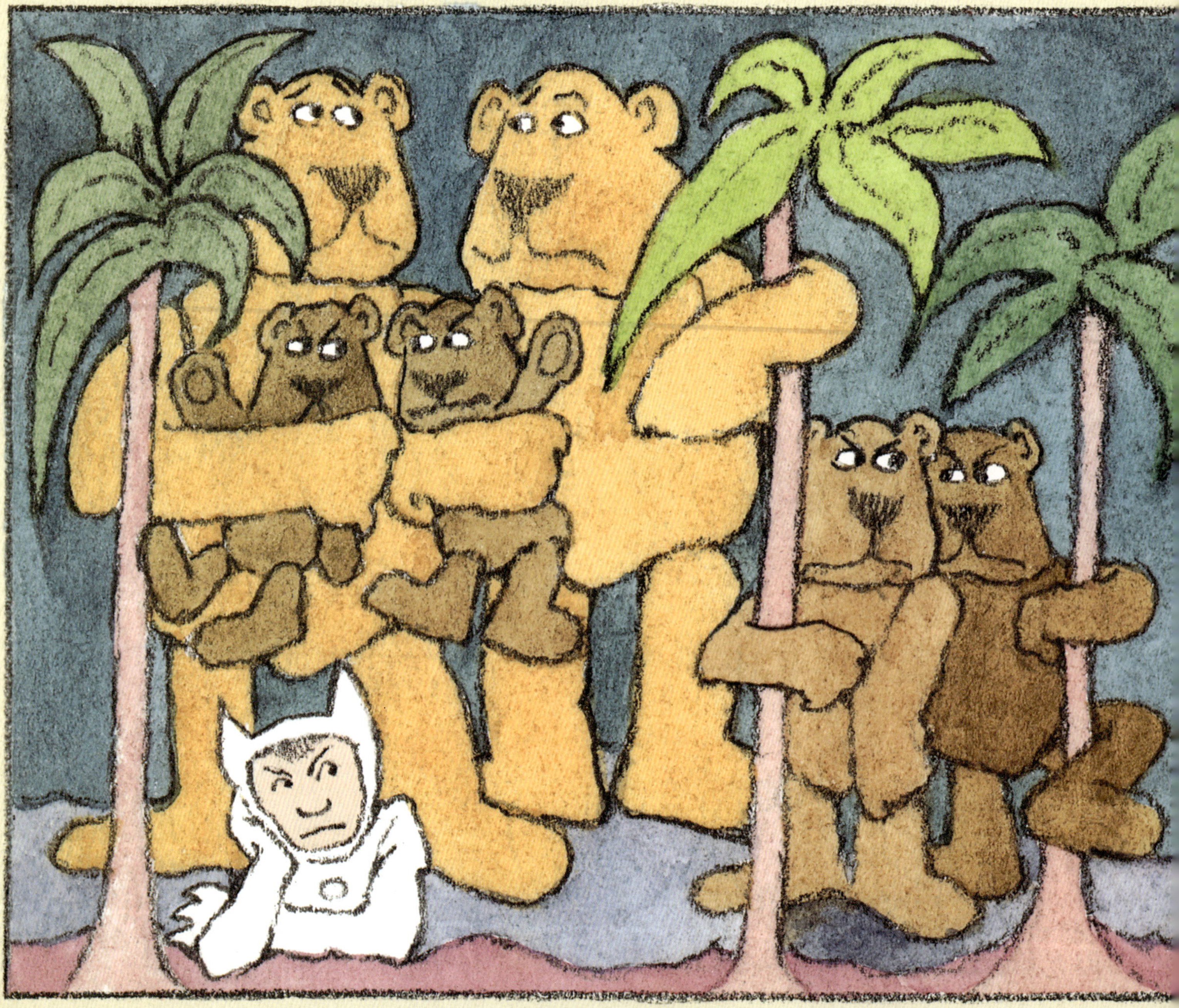

Giving stares

YUM

Collecting fares

Stepping in

squares

million

aires

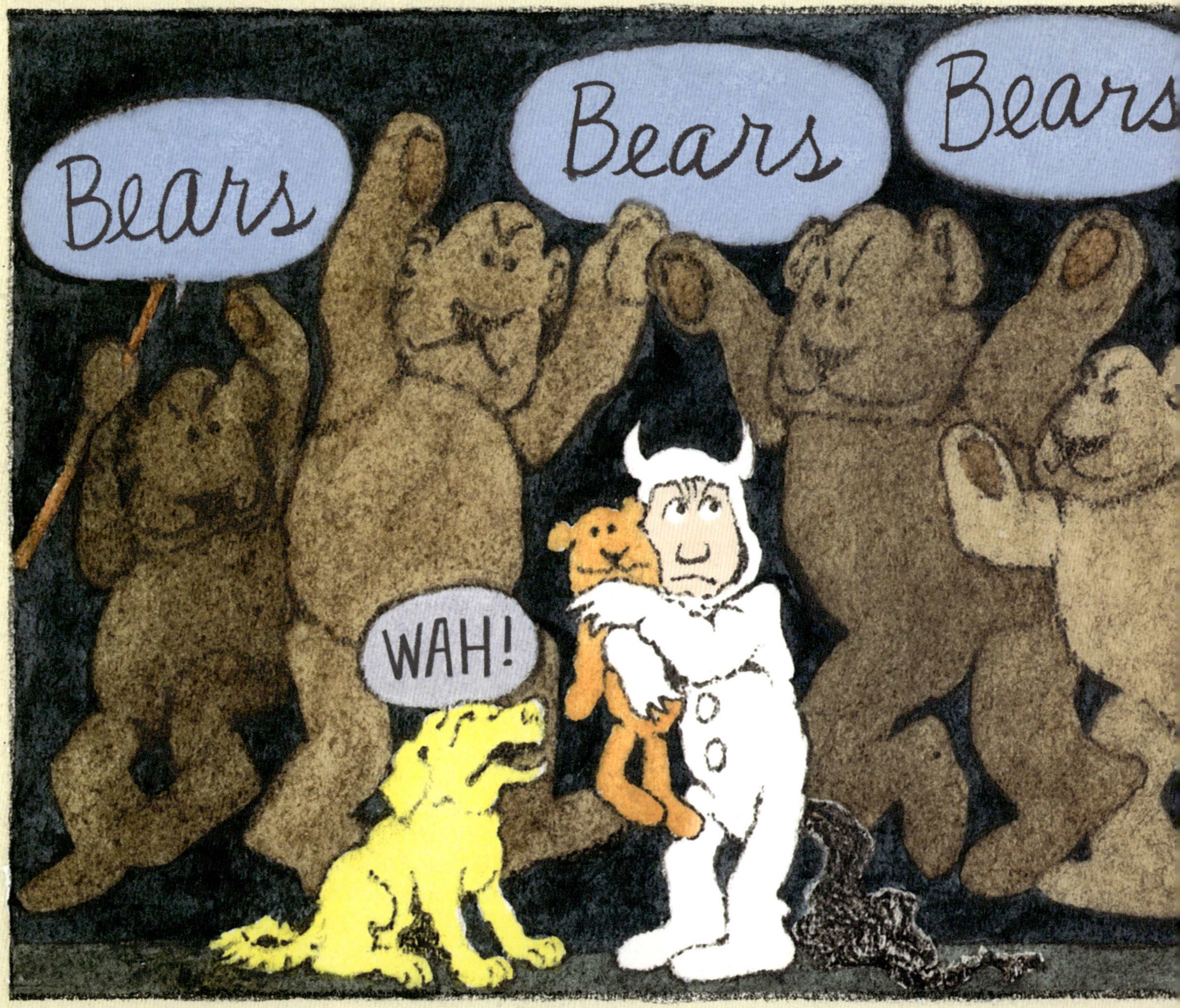
Bears
Bears
Bears
WAH!

every

wheres

Text copyright © 1948 by Ruth Krauss,
copyright renewed 1976 by Ruth Krauss
Pictures copyright © 2005 by Maurice Sendak
Hand lettering by Tom Starace
Library of Congress control number: 2004105682
Ruth Krauss's text for BEARS, with pictures by Phyllis Rowand,
was first published in 1948 by Harper & Brothers

Michael di Capua Books · HarperCollins Publishers